lonely planet

NOT-FOR-PARENTS

AFRICA
Everything you ever wanted to know

Clive Gifford

D0549783

CONTENTS

THIS BOOK'S A BLAST.

HELLO! VERY PLEASED TO EAT YOU.

PHARAOH'S A JOLLY GOOD FELLOW.

NOT-FOR-PARENTS

THIS IS NOT A GUIDEBOOK. And it is definitely Not-for-Parents.

IT IS THE REAL INSIDE STORY about one of the world's most exciting continents – Africa. In this book you'll hear fascinating tales about **Dogon warriors**, fearless explorers, Nollywood film stars, **crazy coffins**, Egyptian tombs and **witch doctors**.

Check out cool stories about **Tuareg nomads**, the world's biggest diamond, killer crocodiles and eccentric dictators. You'll find thumb pianos and mummified monkeys, **camel caravans**, a golden death mask, a seriously tough desert race and **history** galore.

This book shows you an **AFRICA** your parents probably don't even know about.

Sand, sand and more sand

The mighty Sahara Desert covers approximately a tenth of the continent. It's bigger than Brazil and only a little smaller than the entire United States. Africa's official hottest temperature was recorded in the Saharan oasis of Kebili in Tunisia – a sweltering 55°C (131°C)!

Morocco

Alger

Western Sahara

180m
(590 ft)
The height of the tallest sand dunes in the Sahara Desert.

Mauritania

Cape Verde

Senegal

Gambia

Guinea–Bissau

Guinea

Mali

Burkina Faso

Benin

Sierra Leone

Ivory Coast

Ghana

Togo

Liberia

Equatorial Guinea

Fearsome frogs

Africa is home to many of the biggest animals and as frogs go, the goliath frog from Cameroon is a whopper. Measuring up to 33cm (13in) long, this enormous amphibian can weigh 3.3kg (7.3lb) and can cover 3m (10ft) in a single hop.

This goliath frog weighs in at almost 3kg (6.6lb).

EXTREME CONTINENT

Welcome to Africa, the world's wildest continent! Africa is a continent of extremes, from lush, moist rainforest and snow-capped mountain peaks to the world's largest hot desert and bone-dry grasslands. Packed with vast natural riches including gold and diamonds, it is also home to many of the world's poorest people.

Going underground

Inside the forbiddingly named Dragon's Breath Cave, in Namibia, lies the world's largest underwater lake. It sits 100m (328ft) below ground and is the size of two soccer pitches.

Lake Malawi has the most freshwater fish species in the world – as many as 1000.

TALLEST PEAK

Mount Kilimanjaro in Tanzania is a massive dormant volcano. It stands 5895m (19,340ft) tall, making it the highest point in Africa. It is home to Africa's only ice glacier.

1470m (4822ft)
The depth of Lake Tanganyika in east Africa. It's the continent's deepest lake.

Short stuff
Deep in the Ituri Forest of Central Africa live the Mbuti people. Adults rarely grow taller than 1.45m (5ft), making them amongst the shortest people on Earth.

Tunisia
Libya
Egypt
Niger
Chad
Sudan
Eritrea
Djibouti
Ethiopia
Algeria
Central African Republic
South Sudan
Cameroon
Somalia
Congo
Uganda
Kenya
Gabon
Democratic Republic of Congo
Rwanda
Burundi
Tanzania
Angola
Malawi
Zambia
Mozambique
Madagascar
Mauritius
Zimbabwe
Namibia
Botswana
Swaziland
South Africa
Lesotho

WANT MORE?

More facts ☆ www.ducksters.com/geography/africa.php

RUSH HOUR

Beep! Beep! Out of the way. These busy beasts are on a mission to reach new grazing grounds on the Serengeti plains. Every year, close to two million mammals make the long-distance circular journey, from north Tanzania to southwest Kenya, in search of fresh grasslands.

The herds of animals travel around 1600km (994mi) each year on their journey

Spot the zebras among the wildebeest.

450,000
The approximate number of baby wildebeest born on the migration.

RAINS ON THE PLAIN

Rains hit the plains of the Serengeti in November and December, sparking plant growth. Vast herds of grazers scoff as much as they can. In January and February, they give birth to young. By April, they begin to head northwest.

Return journey
After chomping their way through the grasslands of the northern Serengeti, the herds head further north to reach the Mara plains by July. They stay there until October, then begin the long trek south again to the Serengeti.

August
September
July
October
June
November
May
Serengeti National Park
April
December
January
March
February

MMM, LUNCH!

Hyena

RISKY ROUTE

On the way there and back, the huge herds face a number of threats. These include thirst, starvation or falls as they make treacherous jumps and scramble up and down steep banks. Lions, leopards, crocodiles and hyenas lay in wait for any members of the herds who stray too close to them.

MIGRATION TRAFFIC WATCH

Wildebeest 1.3 million

Gazelles 360,000

Zebras 190,000

Elands 12,000

250,000
The number of wildebeest that die during their travels every year.

Each front hoof of a wildebeest leaves a trail of scent for others to follow.

WANT MORE?

See the movement of the herd ☆ www.eyesonafrica.net/migration.htm

WE'RE HAVING MARY FOR DINNER

Mary fell in love with Africa, particularly the Fang people whom she found intelligent and loyal. Staying in one Fang hut, she identified a horrible smell coming from a bag hanging from the roof. It contained a mixture of shrivelled and fresh human body parts. Urgh!

DANGER! Burly sailors and villagers threaten Mary. She gives them tobacco or wards them off with a wave of her revolver.

Fang men of N'Tem

Wooden mask of the Fang tribe

MMMM! NOW THAT IS ONE TASTY LADY.

DANGER! Leopard attacks. Mary sees it off with a chair and then smashes a water jug over its head.

River deep, mountain high

Apart from living with a cannibal tribe and exploring dense jungle, Mary canoed down the crocodile-infested Ogooué River in Gabon. She was also one of the first foreigners to climb the 4040m-high Mount Cameroon volcano (13,255ft). What a gal!

DANGER! Hostile cannibal tribe threatens to kill and eat Mary. She wins them over with trades, a friendly smile and by helping to treat the sick.

FANGS FOR THE MEMORIES

Mary Henrietta Kingsley (1862–1900) was a dutiful daughter in Victorian England. She lived with her ill parents until they both died in 1892. In her 30s, with next-to-no schooling or travel experience, Mary was expected to live at home alone. So, what could be more surprising than her heading off to explore mysterious and dangerous West Africa? Not to mention living with the Fang tribe who, at the time, were cannibals!

THIS LADY'S NOT FOR TASTING!

STAKES AND SNAKES

Mary's prim and proper clothing, particularly her thick skirt, saved her life when she fell into a deep pit filled with sharp stakes. While exploring the thick forests of West Africa, she was forced to eat big snakes, roasted over a fire, which she declared better than some of the other grub on offer.

DANGER! Killer croc clambers into Mary's canoe! She gives the 2.5m-long croc (8ft) a hefty whack of her paddle on its snout.

DANGER! Hippos block Mary's path. She gives them a fierce prod with her umbrella to move them out of the way.

Something fishy
Mary was no scientist. Yet she returned to England with samples of fish, a snake and insects unknown to science at the time – a stunning achievement.

'Being human, she must have been afraid of something, but one never found out what it was.'

– Quote from *Jungle Book* writer Rudyard Kipling, who met Mary in Africa when she returned in 1900 to work as a nurse.

WANT MORE?

Mary wrote two books that taught Europeans much about African customs.

INDEPENDENCE DAY

Imagine an entire continent controlled by foreign countries. That was Africa over 100 years ago when almost all of its land was ruled from afar by countries in Europe. By 1945, only four African countries – Ethiopia, Liberia, South Africa and Egypt – were independent, but boy was there a rush afterwards…

Freedom fighters
Sudan, Morocco and Tunisia became free in 1956. These were followed by dozens more nations over the next 25 years, but many people had to fight long and hard, trying non-violent protests and sometimes resorting to violence, before they won their freedom.

Slaving away
Liberia was founded by freed slaves from the United States who first settled there in the 1820s. Its capital, Monrovia, is named after the fifth US president, James Monroe.

17
The number of countries that became independent in 1960 – a bumper year!

Splitting up
This bronze statue was a gift to the nation of Zambia (which gained its independence in 1964) from its first president, Kenneth Kuanda. It symbolizes breaking the chains of foreign control.

In 1961, Julius Nyerere celebrates independence for Tanzania after becoming its first leader.

Freedom Statue, Lusaka, Zambia.

Bronze heights

This whopper (taller than the US Statue of Liberty) commemorates Senegal's 50 years of independence from France. It was actually built by North Koreans.

African Renaissance Monument

CAN'T WAIT TO PUT MY ARMS DOWN!

JOURNEY TO INDEPENDENCE

South Sudan (from Sudan) 2011

Eritrea (from Ethiopia) 1993

Namibia (from South Africa) 1990

Djibouti (from France) 1977

Mozambique (from Portugal) 1975

Equatorial Guinea (from Spain) 1968

Kenya (from Britain) 1963

Algeria (from France) 1962

Burundi (from Belgium) 1962

Benin (from France) 1960

Ghana (from Britain) 1957

Libya (from Italy) 1951

Newest nations

After a long struggle, Eritrea broke free of Ethiopia in 1993. For 18 years it was Africa's youngest independent country. Then, in 2011, following a referendum where over 98% of people said yes, South Sudan split from Sudan to become Africa's newest nation.

South Sudanese people go wild as they celebrate their country's first birthday

"Happy Birthday to us!!

Ethiopia is the only African country that avoided becoming a colony, despite Italian forces invading in the 1930s.

WANT MORE?

I WANT MY MUMMY!

Vulture amulet

Scarab beetle lucky charm

That's a wrap
The body was wrapped in many metres of linen bandages. Amulets and other lucky charms were tucked inside the linen.

You've got to hand it to the ancient Egyptians. When they wanted something preserved, they did a grand job. By removing all moisture from a dead human body and wrapping it up, some of their mummies have survived 5000 years. Over the past 400 years, many mummies have been rediscovered and dug up to become all the rage among wealthy collectors.

I FEEL A BIT LIGHT HEADED!

Brain drain
Using a metal hook up the hooter, the brain was mashed up and then pulled out of the skull through the nostrils. It was then thrown away.

No guts
Lungs, intestines, stomach and liver were all removed via a slit in the body. These were stored in special jars.

Salt and prepare
The body was covered in natron (a salt-like substance) and left to dry out for 40 days. Expensive perfumed oils were rubbed into the skin because the deceased was worth it!

Mummy encased inside painted coffin.

Flying pharaoh
In 1974, the fungus-riddled mummy of Pharaoh Ramesses II was flown from Egypt to France for treatment. He had to be issued with a real passport. It gave his job as 'King (deceased)!'

Ramesses II

> IT'S TOO LATE. I'VE BEEN DEAD FOR CENTURIES!

Mummy entering an MRI scanner.

Undercover search
Ancient Egyptian mummies are being discovered all the time. Scientists give some a full-on medical body scan to try to work out how they died.

The embalming table was sloped to let all the body juices run away from the body. Yuk!

FIVE USES OF A DEAD MUMMY

1. Ground up to form Caledonian brown or mummy brown oil paint for 17–19th century artists.

2. Mummy's linen was used as unique gift wrap by Europeans.

 3. Ground-up mummy was taken as a tea or potion by royalty to improve health.

4. Party entertainment. A mummy unwrapping was the highlight of a posh party in Victorian times.

5. Some mummies were pounded into a pulp and spread on farm fields as fertiliser.

WANT MORE?

Mummies ☆ www.pbs.org/wgbh/nova/ancient/afterlife-ancient-egypt.html

MAN V CHEETAH

In 2007, South African rugby superstar Bryan Habana faced an unusual showdown. Habana was one of the fastest men in world rugby. He could sprint 100m (328ft) in under 11 seconds. Yet he didn't stand a chance against Cetane – a young female cheetah. Even with a 30m (98ft) head start, Cetane powered past Bryan to reach the finish line in just a few strides.

Big nostrils to funnel in lots of air

Long legs propelled by massive leg muscles.

IF I DON'T BEAT HIM, I'LL EAT HIM!

3
The number of strides a cheetah needs to go from zero to 60km/h (37mph) That's fast!

Cheetahs run flat out to catch a young gazelle.

TAKE A BREAK

Cheetahs mostly prey on smaller antelope and gazelles. They hunt during the day by sight, stalking until they are 10–40m (33–131ft) away before sprinting. They hope to outrun their prey within just a few hundred metres. Beyond that distance, they quickly get puffed out and need a rest.

Cuddly cubs
Ahh, cute aren't they? Cheetah cubs live with their mums for the first 18 to 24 months. This protects them when they are most vulnerable to hungry lions and hyenas.

What makes a cheetah so fast, the fastest land animal on the planet?

Safe breeding

Bryan raced Cetane at the Ann van Dyk Cheetah Centre. It's a conservation centre that helps to protect cheetahs. Over 800 cubs have been reared there since 1971.

Large heart and lungs to pump oxygen-rich blood around the body fast.

Ridged footpads and semi-retractable claws grip just like running shoes.

Flexible spine acts as a spring, adding power to each stride.

Long tail helps with balance when turning at high speed.

Small, aerodynamic head cuts through the air.

UNDER THREAT

Cheetah numbers have fallen almost as fast as they run. There were as many as 120,000 cheetahs in 1900. Today, there are less than 15,000 in the wild. Most of these live in the southern and eastern grasslands of Africa.

WANT MORE?

More cheetah info ☆ www.cheetah.org/?nd=cheetah_facts

Camel convoy

In late autumn, Tuareg tribespeople set off in camel caravans across the harsh, dry Tenere Desert in Niger. They load their camels with hay for them to graze on. They also carry cheese, dried beans and vegetables to trade with the Kanuri people who collect salt in Bilma, north-east Niger.

> The journey takes three weeks but there's no time to rest. The caravan heads further south to sell the salt at major markets in Niger and Nigeria.

20,000
The number of camels in a single caravan in the past, stretching for 25km (16mi) across the desert.

SALT OF THE EARTH

Next time you reach for the salt, remember you're pouring 'white gold' onto your grub. That's the nickname salt had in the past when traders got filthy rich on the proceeds of giant camel caravans transporting salt in blocks across African deserts. Though on a much smaller scale, the same centuries-old trade is still carried out today.

Head of the herd

There are no road signs in the desert, so caravans depend on their madagu, or headman, to lead them accurately. The caravan will typically cover 50km (31mi) a day. As soon as they stop at night, the camels are unloaded and dinner is prepared. Don't get excited – it's boiled millet – a grainy porridge.

Filthy job
This Tuareg youngster drew the short straw when jobs were handed out. He's got to collect camel dung, which will be burnt for a night-time fire.

SALT WORKS

When the Tuareg reach Bilma they trade with the Kanuri. The Kanuri gather salt by digging deep pits and letting the hot summer Sun evaporate water to leave a thick layer of salt behind. The salt is then cut into slabs.

NO MORE... OR I'M REALLY GOING TO GET THE HUMP!

Some salt at Bilma is cut into smaller 2kg (4lb) cakes called 'fochi'.

Each camel is loaded with 200kg (440lb) of salt.

Richest man in the world!
King of the Malian Empire, Mansa Musa (1280–1337) controlled half of the world's known salt supply. He was thought to be worth more than £262 billion (US$400 billion)! On a trip to Mecca, he handed out hundreds of gold bars to poor people he met on the way. What a guy!

After leaving Bilma, the Tuareg transport the salt south. At the salt markets, they haggle hard to get the best price for their wares.

WANT MORE?
Salt route ☆ www.bradshawfoundation.com/africa/tuareg_salt_caravans/index.php

WAY TO GO!

To the Ga-Adangbe people of Ghana and parts of Togo, death isn't the end. They believe the deceased person goes on to a new life in the next world where they are more powerful than before. The Ga-Adangbe believe that the dead can influence the lives of the living. So, to keep them sweet, friends and relatives shell out for the most extreme coffins on the planet.

I'M DYING FOR SOME WATER...

One of about twelve coffin makers in Teshie and other suburbs of Accra, Ghana's capital city

CARVING OUT A LIVING

Coffins are carved and built by skilled carpenters in small workshops. The coffins are shaped and styled using traditional woodworking tools. Often there are no plans, only photos of the real objects as a guide. An epic paint job usually finishes them off in style.

Star for a day
Completed coffins are often kept hidden under a cloth wrap until the day of the funeral. All that hard work is soon buried.

Funeral procession in Ghana

BUT IS IT ART?

Yes! The work of Ghana's coffin designers has been exhibited in art galleries all over the world. In 2000, the British Museum bought an eagle coffin by Paa Joe, one of Ghana's leading coffin makers.

A frilled-lizard coffin made in Ghana for an Australian festival.

> I JUST CAN'T STOP COFFIN'!

Casket case

Paa Joe puts the finishing touches to a Mercedes-Benz coffin. Joe hopes the relatives of the deceased, a keen driver, will be dead proud.

£520 (US$800)

Cost of the most expensive coffin designs in Accra, Ghana.

Designs for the departed

Coffin designs from just one of the workshops include:

Mobile phones
Trainers
Lions
Jet aircraft
Crabs
Cruise ship
Pineapples
Robot
Soft drink bottles
Referee's whistle

WORK AND PLAY

Some coffins are designed to reflect the dead person's job, such as this giant fish for a fisherman. Others may be in the form of a car for a taxi driver, a chicken for a farmer or a camera for a photographer. Designs may be modelled on the deceased's favourite animal or interest – from a lion to a musical instrument.

WANT MORE?

See more amazing coffins ☆ www.bbc.co.uk/news/world-africa-11879532

Greenpoint Stadium, Capetown, South Africa.

Passion play
Football is exciting to play and needs only simple equipment. It's played anywhere and everywhere in Africa, even if the teams don't have a proper ball.

NUMBER ONE

Football is played and followed throughout Africa – from the north (Morocco, Algeria and Tunisia took part in the continent's first regional competition in 1919) to the south (South Africa became the first African nation to host the World Cup in 2010). The sport is Africa's number one team game.

WISH WE HAD SOME GRASS ON OUR PITCH!

Makeshift balls are made from plastic bags and string, or rags and leaves stitched together.

Cup of Nations
This tournament began with just three teams (Egypt, Ethiopia and Sudan) in 1957, but has boomed since. In 2013, 47 nations battled away in qualifying games to take part in the 16-team tournament. It is Africa's biggest football event and attracts huge crowds live and on TV.

ON THE BALL

With names like 'Naughty Boys' and 'Botswana Meat Commission', Africa's unusual football club names might inspire a snigger or two. But the passion of African fans and the quality of African footballers is no joke. And when it comes to staging a soccer spectacle, Africans are world beaters.

49%
of all the players at the 2012 African Cup of Nations played for clubs in Europe not Africa.

OI REF, HAVE YOU SEEN MY GLASSES?

Golden boy
Yaya Touré grew up in poverty in Ivory Coast. But when he signed with Manchester City in 2010, he earned a weekly wage of £185,000 (US$280,000) plus bonuses! In contrast, the average worker in Ivory Coast earns a little over £1000 (US$1500) per year.

ON THE BALL

Founded in 2006, Vakhegula Vakhegula (meaning 'Grannies' in the Xitsonga language) is a club of 40 grandmothers. Aged from 40 to 80 plus, they play casual games of football in South Africa.

CURIOUS CLUB NAMES

Mysterious Dwarfs
(Ghana)

Eleven Men in Flight
(Swaziland)

Golf Leopards
(Sierra Leone)

Killer Giants
(Botswana)

WANT MORE?

A grasshopper fast food stall in Uganda.

YOU'VE GOT YOUR BUGS, NOW HOP OFF!

Munching on grasshoppers

Giant African snail

Tasty bug nibbles

STRANGE SNACKS

Africa is home to some seriously out-there dishes and surreal snacks. These range from snake meat on skewers and dried antelope meat (known as biltong) to warthog ribs, roasted crocodile and giant African snails as big as your fist.

LOW-COST LOCUST

Cooked bugs are all the rage in parts of Africa. Plentiful and full of protein, they're often eaten after being boiled or deep fried. Market stalls in many African towns sell fried termites, locusts and grasshoppers by the scoopful.

60%
The amount of protein in a mopane worm – almost twice as much as beef!

When is a worm not a worm?
When it's a mopane worm! These are actually giant caterpillars, found in Zimbabwe, Namibia and other parts of Southern Africa. They feast on the leaves of the mopane tree. Highly nutritious, they are collected and dried out in the sun to form a tasty, crispy snack by themselves or cooked in a dish.

Most of the guts of the mopane worm can be squeezed out with a sharp press of your fingers. Urgh!

Eggs-iting omelette
Insects not your thing? No matter. How about an ostrich-egg omelette? It's no yoke. Especially when you consider that a single egg can weigh well over 1kg (2.2lb), and can make enough omelette to feed up to 12 people.

An ostrich protecting its eggs in South Africa.

60
The minutes needed to boil an ostrich egg. Fried is faster!

CATERPILLAR CRUNCH RECIPE

1. Soak dried mopane worms in water for 4 hours.

2. Fry onions, tomatoes, chilli and ginger.

3. Add worms and cook for 5-15 minutes.

4. Serve on a bed of cornmeal porridge.

Preparing an ostrich-egg omelette.

Ostrich egg

Chicken egg

WANT MORE?

Eating bugs ☆ www.scienceinafrica.com/old/index.php?q=2003/october/stinkbug.htm

SHAKA ATTACK!

Born in 1787, Shaka was just six years old when his father, Senzangakhona, chieftain of a small Zulu clan, banished him and his mother. They went to live with other tribes, including the Elangeni who treated them very badly. Shaka never forgot this as he united the south African Zulu peoples, and turned them into a formidable fighting force. Shaka was assassinated in 1828.

MAJOR CHANGES

Shaka rose to power in his 20s and, once in control, gave his army a complete overhaul. He introduced new weapons, sneaky tactics and training drills to bash his soldiers into shape.

SHAKA TACTICS

Shaka's armies lined up for battle in a 'bull-horn' formation.

Enemy

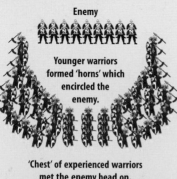

Younger warriors formed 'horns' which encircled the enemy.

'Chest' of experienced warriors met the enemy head on.

'Loins' of reserve soldiers could move forward to replace fallen members of the 'chest'.

Behind the barriers

Large, heavy cowhide shields protected most of the body. They could be locked together in a row to protect the front line of advancing warriors.

Shaka, king of the Zulus.

Long throwing spears called *assegai* were used for long-distance warfare.

MMM, I'LL DEAL WITH YOU IN A MINUTE!

Apprentice warriors, called ubidi, were trained from as young as six to carry food and supplies.

BUILDING A KINGDOM

Shaka's forces defeated local clans and absorbed their warriors into his army. Numbers grew from around 200 to more than 20,000. He built a new capital, KwaBulawayo, for his kingdom. It contained 1400 huts for the royal household alone.

Extreme revenge!

Shaka ordered Elangeni tribe members who had bullied him as a child to be impaled on sharp sticks. He also locked an enemy's mother in a hut with jackals and hyenas. Once they had eaten her, he had the hut burned down. Brutal!

The punishment for any warrior losing his iklwa spear was death!

7000
The number of people Shaka had executed for not mourning enough at the death of his mother.

One metre-long stabbing spears (3ft) called iklwa were powerful weapons in close-combat fighting.

GET THE MAN BUT MIND THE HORSE!

WANT MORE?

See Shakaland, a Zulu theme park in South Africa ☆ www.shakaland.ahagroup.co.za

THE BIG FIVE

Take aim… fire! Meet the fashionable Big Five – Cape buffalo, elephant, leopard, lion and rhinoceros. In the past, these were the African animals to hunt. Today, tourists have mostly swapped their hunting rifles for digicams and smartphones to shoot these photogenic creatures with.

HONESTLY, IT'S JUST AS WELL I'M THICK SKINNED…

Charge account
Available in both black and white, rhinos are giant-sized herbivores. They crush the scales at almost 1.5 tonnes (1.7 tons). As some unfortunate hunters learned to their cost, that weight charging at top speeds of over 50km/h (31mph) is to die for.

Feline groovy
Spots are always in vogue for the leopard. It eats anything from beetles to antelopes. Leopards tend to stalk their prey silently and strangle them with a killer bite to their throat.

Well built
Strictly XXXL, male elephants can stand 4m (13ft) tall at the shoulder. They come with the most versatile of accessories – a long, prehensile nose containing over 40,000 muscles. These trunks are used for breathing, drinking, trumpeting calls and as a feeding tool.

3600
The estimated number of black rhinos left in the wild in Africa.

HOW COME I HAVE TO WEAR THE HORNS?

Hot to trot
Cape buffalo are no skinny size 6 supermodels. They weigh up to 850kg (1874lb) and have 50mm-thick skin (2in). Their sharp horns and sudden charges at humans have given them the nickname of 'the widow maker' amongst big-game hunters.

THE MANE EVENT
Check out the undoubted king and queen of the catwalk. Lions rock a tufted tail and hairy head (mane) unique amongst the large felines. Lions like to say it loud and proud – their roar can be heard more than 6km (4mi) away.

WANT MORE?

Lionesses do most of the hunting in a pride, as well as rearing their cubs.

Dr Christiaan Barnard

Dr Michael DeBakey

Two months before his pioneering heart transplant, Christiaan had performed the first kidney transplant in South Africa.

GUYS, IT'S TIME WE HAD A HEART-TO-HEART TALK.

HEART TO HEART

In December 1967, South African surgeon Dr Christiaan Barnard went into work one Saturday, unknown to the world. He came out on the Monday as a global superstar. Barnard had just performed the world's first-ever heart transplant in Cape Town's Groote Schuur Hospital.

TREK TO SUCCESS

Born in poverty, Christiaan had four brothers. One of them, Abraham, died aged five of heart failure. As a student, Christiaan walked 8km (5mi) each day to study medicine at Cape Town University. In the 1950s, whilst studying surgical techniques in the USA, he washed cars and did odd jobs to make money.

WOOF... AND... WOOF!

In the 1960s, Barnard performed heart transplant experiments on dogs. He also surgically added a second head to one dog. Horrible!

Dr Adrian
Kantrowitz

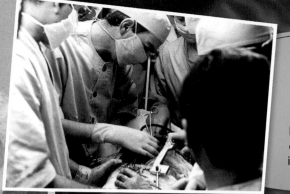

The first transplant
In 1967, South African
grocer Louis Washkansky was
dying of severe heart problems.
In a tense nine-hour operation
Barnard transplanted the heart
of a female car crash victim
into Washkansky's chest.

Electric shocks were needed
to start the new heart.

Operation heart beat
After the transplant operation, Louis
Washkansky's new heart beat strongly.
But sadly he died 18 days later. Barnard
persevered and his second patient, Philip
Blaiberg, survived for 19½ months.
Dirk van Zyl, his 6th patient, lived for
23 years after receiving a new heart.

Philip Blaiberg and his
wife leaving Groote Schuur
Hospital in Capetown.

New lease of life
Today, over 3800 heart
transplants are performed
worldwide. Many patients
go on to live active lives after
surgery. In 2001, for example, Kelly
Perkins climbed Tanzania's giant
Mount Kilimanjaro, six years after
receiving a new heart.

WANT
MORE?

The first heart transplant ☆ www.heartofcapetown.co.za/timeline%205.htm

Mystery stone cone
A conical tower of power for the ruler of Great Zimbabwe. What was it used for?

All the buildings and walls of Great Zimbabwe were made without cement or mortar – just millions of stones placed together ever so carefully.

Karl Mauch (1837–75)

THE MYSTERY OF GREAT ZIMBABWE

Rumours of a giant stone city in central southern Africa floated around the continent long before 1871, when young German explorer Karl Mauch stumbled upon a massive set of ruins. Great Zimbabwe, as the local Shona people called it, would both name a country and provide archaeologists with an enduring mystery.

BIG DEAL

The ruins of Great Zimbabwe are the biggest set of ancient structures found south of the Sahara. Towers stand over 20m (66ft) tall. Some walls are 11m (36ft) high and stretch for hundreds of metres.

LOOK! HERE WE ARE, DOWN HERE!

BLUNDERING AMATEURS

At first, white Europeans tried to disprove Great Zimbabwe was built by black Africans. They sent amateur expeditions, but they destroyed much of the archaeological evidence that may have solved the mysteries of the sensational stone city.

Zimbabwe's national flag features the bird sculptures found at the ruins.

Who built it?
All the evidence points to an African tribe. Many, including the Lemba, Shona and Venda peoples, claim their ancestors were responsible, but no one really knows.

How did it grow so rich?
Was it a trading centre? Did its people conquer others, or was it a religious centre that people paid to have built?

18,000
Great Zimbabwe's peak population somewhere between the 12th and 15th centuries.

The walls were almost 5m (16ft) thick in places.

Why was it abandoned?
Surely its massive walls didn't let in invaders, so what happened? Perhaps there was no food in the area or the trade it relied on went elsewhere?

Awesomely massive stone walls gave the centre of Great Zimbabwe no way through for invaders.

GREAT TRADE
Many historians believe that the town was the centre of a great cattle, gold and ivory trading empire. It's thought to have had links as far afield as the Middle East and Asia. Glass from Arabia, gold from Persia and porcelain from China have all been found at the ruins.

WANT MORE?

More ☆ www.pbs.org/wgbh/nova/ancient/mysteries-of-great-zimbabwe.html

BAREFOOT RUNNERS

At the 2010 Rome Marathon, Ethiopia's Siraj Gena was leading the men's race when he took off his shoes and ran the last 300m (984ft) in his bare feet. His victory commemorated the 50 years since another memorable race in Rome, also made by a barefooted Ethiopian athlete.

OOH, MY FEET! WISH I'D BOUGHT THOSE TRAINERS.

Abebe Bikila broke the Olympic marathon record by over eight minutes.

Between races, Bikila worked as a bodyguard to the Ethiopian emperor, Haile Selassie.

ABEBE BIKILA

As they lined up to race the 1960 Olympic marathon, some competitors sniggered at the unknown barefooted Ethiopian amongst them. Two and a quarter hours later, they'd stopped smirking when Abebe Bikila became the first black African athlete to win an Olympic gold medal. He repeated the feat four years later – the first person to win the marathon twice.

HAILE GEBRSELASSIE

Some of the greatest-ever medium and long distance runners have come from Africa. Many, such as Haile Gebrselassie, started their careers running barefoot. Gebrselassie used to run to school and back again from his family's farm in Asella, Ethiopia. He ran 20km (12mi) every day – nearly a half-marathon!

UH-OH, I CAN'T SLOW DOWN!

27
The number of world records Haile Gebrselassie broke throughout his athletics career.

Bookish runner
Gebrselassie's unusual running style, with a crooked left arm, came from running to and from school with his books clamped under his arm.

Kenya's Caroline Chepkurui Tuigong wins the World Junior 3000m (2mi) race in Beijing, running barefoot.

ZOLA BUDD

Born and brought up in South Africa, Zola was just 17 when she broke the world record for the women's 5000m (3mi). She ran barefoot even at the 1984 Olympics, where she clashed with US favourite Mary Decker. Both finished out of the medals, although Budd did win gold at the World Cross-Country Championships in 1985 and 1986.

Barefoot today
Many young Africans cannot afford expensive running shoes. Some elite athletes still prefer running barefoot. These include Sarah Abu Hassan from Egypt and Margaret Muriuki from Kenya.

WANT MORE?

Learn more about Bikila ☆ www.abebebikila11.com

MAN-EATERS

Africa's packed with a whole cavalcade of killers who prey on the foolish and the unwary. These range from tiny but lethal bacteria, viruses and malaria-carrying mosquitoes to giant raging rhinos and deadly hippos. Two species have produced real outlaws – a shocking croc and a pair of man-eating lions.

I WONDER WHERE GUSTAVE'S HIDING THIS TIME...

WANTED

Gustave: AKA the Killer Croc

Species: Nile crocodile

Crimes: Attacks on over 300 humans, many of whom were eaten.

Location: Lake Tanganyika and Ruzizi river, Burundi.

Length: Over 6.1m (20ft) – most crocs are under 5m (16ft).

Age: Over 60

Distinguishing features: Four bullet scars – one on his head and three on his right side.

DEADLY BITE

Still on the loose, the elusive killer croc Gustave stays hidden much of the time. When he launches an attack he uses his powerful jaws filled with over 60 razor-sharp teeth. He has also used his muscular tail to swipe school children into the river before eating them.

A load of old croc
These local villagers seem pretty pleased with themselves after bagging the killer croc of Lake Rukwa in 1950. Gustave, ...

All you can eat

Regular Nile crocodiles mostly feed on fish but will attack and eat zebras, wildebeest, young hippos and humans if they get the chance. They can eat up to a fifth of their bodyweight in a single meal.

Killer cats

In 1898, workers building the Kenya-Uganda railway were savaged by a pair of Tsavo lions. The wild cats hunted at night, dragging men out of their tents before killing and eating them. Lieutenant-Colonel Patterson (right) finally shot them both dead. It took nine bullets to stop the second lion in its tracks!

Roaring success

A 1952 film about the Tsavo lions, called *Bwana Devil*, was the first full-length 3D movie in the United States. It sparked a boom in 3D cinema.

CAN'T WAIT TO SINK MY TEETH INTO YOU!

WANT MORE?

The Tsavo lions killed 35–100 humans during their nine-month killing spree.

WHERE'S DOCTOR DAVE?

It was 1869, and no word had been heard from explorer and missionary Dr David Livingstone for almost four years. Journalist Henry Stanley headed to Africa to track him down. Two years later, Stanley finally met Livingstone at Ujiji, a small Tanzanian village on the banks of Lake Tanganyika.

In 1844, Livingstone survived a lion attack. It shattered his shoulder and arm and left him with 13 bite marks!

DR DAVID LIVINGSTONE (1813–73)

Scottish missionary and explorer

Achievements: First European to see Victoria Falls (which he named), discovered Lake Ngami, explored large areas of Central Africa, campaigned against slave trade.

Failures: Didn't discover source of the Nile River, failed to plot a river route through central Africa.

Health problems in Africa: Malaria, dysentery, pneumonia, teeth falling out, cholera, tropical ulcers, broken bones from lion attack and haemorrhoids.

Stanley and Livingstone spent a month exploring the Rusizi River and Lake Tanganyika.

In 1859, Livingstone left an urgent request for supplies at the mouth of the Zambezi River. His message in a bottle sold at auction in 2004.

Dining out

Shortly before Stanley arrived, Livingstone lost all his supplies and had to rely on the kindness of locals. They were fascinated by his use of a knife and fork so, in return for free food, he had to eat his meals in a public roped-off area!

When Livingstone died, his heart was buried in Zambia. But his body was carried by foot on a nine-month, 1600km (994mi) journey to the coast. From there it was shipped back to Britain.

Adventurers united

After about eight months of searching, Stanley finally found Livingstone. The pair spent the next five months exploring Africa together.

Stanley's real name was John Rowlands. He grew up in a workhouse for the poor.

Stanley overcomes the rapids.

WELL, I'M CERTAINLY NOT QUEEN VICTORIA!

DR LIVINGSTONE, I PRESUME?

SIR HENRY MORTON STANLEY (1841–1904)

Anglo-American journalist and explorer

Achievements: Found Dr Livingstone, surveyed Lake Victoria, explored the treacherous Congo River during an epic 999-day-long expedition.

Failures: Didn't persuade Livingstone to come home from Africa, helped King Leopold II of Belgium gain brutal control of Congo region of Africa.

Health problems in Africa: Malaria, dysentery, starvation and fevers.

46,000km
(28,500mi)
The distance Dr Livingstone explored, mostly on foot, during his explorations in Africa.

WANT MORE?

Stanley finds Livingstone ☆ www.eyewitnesstohistory.com/stanley.htm

Rough living

Most Makoko homes don't have running water or electricity. Toilet plumbing is often a hole in the floor with the waste dumped into the lagoon.

LIFE IN MAKOKO

A small fishing village sprang up on the edge of Lagos Lagoon in the 18th century. Today, over 85,000 people – many Nigerians but also some from Togo and Benin – struggle to survive in the overcrowded slum. Many live just offshore in tiny wooden shacks perched on stilts above the lagoon's dirty waters.

SMELLS FISHY

Nigeria consumes more fish than any other African nation. Most of the Makoko locals fish in the lagoon every morning and evening. They bring their catch to shore where they haggle for a good price.

In 2012, the Nigerian government attempted to clear part of the slum, evicting residents and destroying buildings.

CANOE YOU

Children learn to swim and paddle wooden canoes almost before they can walk. They paddle through the slum, scouring through rubbish tips on the lookout for food, firewood and other useful items.

Paddling home on the Lagos Lagoon.

Children play alongside rubbish in Makoko.

On the waterfront
Makoko's homes perch along the edge of the Lagos Lagoon, which is 50km (31mi) long. Wood for waterfront sawmills floats close by.

SCHOOL'S OUT

Many children in Makoko don't go to school, despite education being free in Nigeria. Those who do, attend schools outside Makoko, where there can be as many as 100 kids per class. Alternatively, parents may pay to send their children to private floating schools.

THIS IS SO SLOW... GO FASTER MUM!

WANT MORE?

Images ☆ www.guardian.co.uk/pictures/image/0,8543,-10105140983,00.html

Arrowheads are made of sharpened bone, stone or iron.

HUNTERS OR GATHERERS

The San don't herd animals or grow crops. Instead, the men go out hunting equipped with poison arrows. The women gather food from the roots, leaves and berries of more than 100 different plants.

DON'T MOVE, THIS IS A STICK-UP!

The tip of an arrow is dipped in poison. It breaks off from the rest of the arrow when it hits the target.

THIRSTY WORK

Bows are sometimes smeared with animal fats to stop them cracking in the hot sun.

Step back into the past with the San people, who have lived in southern Africa for more than 20,000 years. The San's unique way of life has been threatened for centuries by people trying to take their land. Only small numbers of San continue to live traditionally, mostly in the Kalahari Desert where water is scarce.

Fire!
The San start a fire by spinning a fire rod between their hands.

OW, MY BLISTERS ARE KILLING ME!

Attack then track
The poison, taken from the ka or ngwa caterpillar, is lethal but can take hours to work. The hunters have to be patient and fit, tracking the poisoned animal for many hours and kilometres until it dies.

Take a break
San hunters rest standing on one leg and using their bow as a prop whilst tracking antelope.

WATER WORKS

The San never take water for granted. There is almost no surface water where they live, so they have to be ingenious. They may collect water by making a sip well – digging a hole to where the sand is damp and then sucking up moisture using a long hollow grass stem.

A plant root, or tuber, contains water which can be squeezed into the mouth.

Shelling out
The San people use tough ostrich egg shells as water bottles. They pierce them and make a small hole in the top to sip water from. Sometimes they bury eggs full of water deep in the sand to keep them cool for later.

When hungry San hunters chew on a bitter plant known as Hoodia Gordonii, it stops them from feeling hungry for a day or two.

WANT MORE?

How the San live together ☆ www.africapoint.com/newsletters/san-people.htm

This 1882 caricature of Leopold II, king of Belgium, shows off his enormous beard.

OH NO, LEO

In the 1880s, powerful countries in Europe carved up much of Africa. New borders split the traditional lands of African tribes and peoples in two. The Europeans enforced harsh laws and misery on many people in their new colonies. None more so than the king of Belgium, Leopold II (1835–1909).

WHAT DO YOU MEAN, MY BEARD'S TOO BIG?

CENTRAL AFRICA

Congo Free State

70
The number of times that the Congo Free State was bigger than Belgium.

ALL MINE, ALL MINE!

In 1885, after years of persuading others he was a good guy who only wanted the best for Africans, Leo gained a massive region of central Africa. It wasn't for his country, Belgium, but purely for himself. He called it Congo Free State. Never has a name been further from the truth!

With the invention of new goods, such as the air-filled tyre, demand for rubber soared. Leo forced the people of Congo to produce as much of it as possible.

RUBBER COATING

Rubber in Congo was harvested from rainforest vines. Workers had to slash the vines and cover their bodies in the oozing liquid. They then had to return to base where the hardened rubber was scraped off their bodies, along with much of their body hair. Ouch!

Workers softened rubber by giving it a good beating.

Workers were beaten with a chicotte, a whip made of dried hippo skin. Its edges were razor sharp.

FORCE PUBLIQUE PUNISHMENTS

★ Villages burned down
★ Wives held hostage
★ Children killed
★ Hands cut off
★ Workers put in chains

Hostage to fortune

Misery came to any worker or village that failed to collect enough rubber or ivory, or pay the harsh taxes. Leo's brutal police, the Force Publique, would beat, whip and torture them.

Thousands of elephants were killed for their ivory tusks during Leo's rule.

In 1908, Leopold handed Congo over to Belgium. He remained so unpopular that when he died, the following year, his funeral procession was booed.

WANT MORE?

A biography of Leo ★ www.historyaccess.com/leopoldiiofbelgi.html

TOUGHEST RACE ON EARTH

Ever run a long-distance race? How long was it? A mile, 3000m (9843ft), maybe 10k (6mi)? Good on you. Now, imagine running a 42km-long marathon (26mi) through a blazing hot desert, then running that distance each day for six days in a row! You'd also be carrying all your week's food and kit on your back? Now that's TOUGH!

In the long run
Almost 900 runners start the race. They sink ankle-deep in sand as they cross dune after dune of the Sahara Desert. Not everyone finishes!

RACE YOU TO THE TOP!

The start of the 250km (155mi) Sahara Desert 'Marathon des Sables'.

A MARATHON EVENT

First run in 1986, the Marathon des Sables is held in Morocco's Sahara Desert over a distance of about 250km (155mi). Organisers provide tents and up to 12 litres (22 pints) of water per runner each day at checkpoints along the way. Runners have to carry everything else they need.

Blistering heat
There's a scene of carnage in the medical centre at the end of each day. Runners are treated for sunburn, heat exhaustion and muscle injuries – but mostly for blisters on their feet.

Wrong direction

Italian policeman Mauro Prosperi lost his way during a sandstorm in the 1994 race. He ended up running 200km (124mi) in the wrong direction! Hopelessly lost and out of food and water, Mauro survived by drinking his own wee and eating bats before a nomadic Tuareg family found him.

Rocky road

It's not all ploughing through sand, though. Racers have to run up lethally steep rocky outcrops and hills such as the 947m-high Jebel El Otfal (3107ft).

Mad Mauro raced the marathon again, in 1998. This time a stubbed toe stopped him from finishing!

The Ahansal brothers finish in 1st and 2nd place in 2005.

KIT LIST

Amongst the long list of things you must pack for the race are:

18,000+ CALORIES OF FOOD

SUPER-STRONG SUNSCREEN

DISTRESS FLARE

HEAD TORCH

SLEEPING BAG

ANTI-VENOM PUMP FOR REMOVING POISON FROM SCORPION STINGS

Brothers in arms

Lahcen Ahansal (no.1) celebrates as he wins yet another race. The Moroccan marathon machine has bagged 10 victories in this race. His younger brother, Mohammad (no.2), has won it three times.

WANT MORE?

Watch official videos of the race ☆ www.youtube.com/user/marathondsables

THUMB PIANOS AND TALKING DRUMS

Music has been an important part of everyday life in Africa for thousands of years. Music and song were used to celebrate ancestors, to pass on stories and customs from one generation to another and, in the case of talking drums, to send messages and signals to other communities quicker than messengers on foot.

SHAKE, RATTLE AND ROLL

Many African instruments make distinctive percussion sounds. There are dozens of different types of drums, as well as shakers filled with beads or seeds, or with rattling objects attached to their outside.

An axatse makes a tuneful rattling sound when shaken.

DO YOU KNOW ANY LADY GAGA TUNES?

105
The maximum loudness in decibels of a djembe drum – the same as a pneumatic drill!

Drumming up interest
For centuries, west Africans have used talking drums to relay messages to other villages. These hourglass-shaped drums have animal skins at each end. The skins are connected by leather cords. The cords alter the drum pitch when the instrument is squeezed under the player's armpit.

West African talking drum and curved beater.

All thumbs

Thumb pianos are known by many names, including mbira and kalimba, and are found throughout Africa. Springy pieces of wood or metal form tines (prongs) which are plucked with the thumbs. The longer the tine, the deeper the note.

YOU HUM IT AND I'LL STRUM IT.

KORA, BLIMEY

Struggling with six strings on your guitar or four on your violin? How about tackling an instrument with 21 strings? The kora is a cross between a harp and a lute. It's made from a halved calabash gourd with animal hide stretched over the hole and has a 21-stringed neck.

Headbangers!

The Royal Drummers of Burundi beat giant drums carried on their heads. The drums are made from hollowed-out tree trunks.

A kora player in Mali.

The largest akandinda xylophones, found in Uganda and other east African countries, need six people to play one instrument.

WANT MORE?

More ☆ www.moa.wfu.edu/files/2012/04/ShakeRattle-Teachers-Guide.pdf

THAT'S A WRAP!

The ancient Egyptians loved their animals. When pet cats died, for instance, owners would often shave off their own eyebrows to show their grief. Egyptians frequently had their pets and other animals mummified and given the old wrap around!

PET PROJECTS

The Egyptians kept many creatures as pets, from dogs and gazelles to falcons and monkeys. Some of these animals worked for a living. Mongooses were trained to hunt water birds, and baboons climbed trees to pick figs.

Baboon mummy

I'M A BIT TIED UP AT THE MOMENT!

Ibis mummy

Good Thoth

Many animal mummies were created as offerings to the ancient Egyptians' gods. The ibis bird was sacred to Thoth, the god of writing and learning. Thousands of ibis mummies have been unearthed in Saqqara – a huge ancient burial site not far from the Egyptian capital, Cairo.

Some bird mummies were 'fed' with snails, packed in amongst their wrappings.

MUMMY FACTORIES

Some animals were lovingly prepared in the same way as human mummies. But, as demand grew for them, many were mass-produced in large workshops. The dead animals were plunged into a vat of liquid resin, then left to dry and harden. They were then wrapped in linen bandages and decorated before being buried, often inside clay jars.

Feline mummy
Demand for mummies to honour the cat goddess, Bastet, led to some young cats being strangled to fuel the mummy industry.

Cat mummy, 332–330 BC

180,000
The number of cat mummies shipped from Egypt to England in 1890.

AND NOT ONE DROP OF WATER IN SIGHT...

Crocodile mummy
Crocs were mummified and preserved to honour the feared god of water, Sobek.

Mummified crocodile head

Mummified animals included:

* HIPPOS *
* SHREWS *
* FALCONS *
* BULLS *
* JACKALS *
* HAWKS * FISH *
* MONGOOSES *
* SNAKES * RAMS *
* LIONS *

WANT MORE?

Mummies shipped to England in the 1890s were ground up and used as fertiliser.

CELL NUMBER 5

In 1964, Robben Island prison got a new inmate – Nelson Mandela. He was a lawyer and political activist with the African National Congress (ANC). He'd been found guilty of acts against the South African government. Mandela was fighting its policy of apartheid (separating and discriminating against people because of their skin colour). He would spend the next 18 years in that prison, mostly in cell number 5.

Metal plate and cup

No stars
Measuring less than 2m (6.5ft) square, Nelson's cell was zero-star accommodation. The only time he was allowed outdoors was to work.

Robben Island

BLEAK ISLAND

The small and barren Robben Island has a long history. Its miserable past dates back to 1657 when exiles and prisoners were banished there by Cape Town founder Jan van Riebeeck. The island became a leper colony in 1855. Later, it was a lunatic asylum before it became a maximum security prison. Today, it's a World Heritage Site.

A TYPICAL DAY ON ROBBEN ISLAND

5.30: Guards wake you up. Breakfast is corn porridge.

6.45: Allowed out of cell to empty toilet bucket.

7.00: Start work in silence, breaking rocks with hammers and chisels.

12.00: Brief lunch of boiled corn.

16.00: Finish work and have ice-cold shower as there is no hot water.

16.30: Dinner of porridge, sometimes with rotting carrot or beetroot added.

20.00: No talking among inmates allowed.

Toilet

Bed

Read all about it

The harsh regime didn't break Mandela. If anything, he grew stronger – even when he was caught writing part of his autobiography, *Long Walk to Freedom*, and banned from being able to read in his cell for four years! In 1982, he was moved to another prison and the campaign to release him grew in the 1980s.

Nelson shows how he broke up rocks while in prison.

Mandela celebrates his 90th birthday at home in Qunu, 2008.

1
The number of visitors that Nelson Mandela was allowed in a year. The visit lasted just 30 minutes.

HOORAY, NO CORN PORRIDGE TODAY!

FREEDOM!

On 11 February 1990, Nelson Mandela was released. He was 71 years old but had no plans to put his feet up. Nelson wanted to see the world. He met hundreds of leaders and celebrities and won the 1993 Nobel Peace Prize. He helped dismantle apartheid and was elected president of South Africa in 1994. Mandela did not use his power to gain revenge. Instead, he tried to bring his country together. This is why he is known fondly as 'Tata', meaning father, by many South Africans.

WANT MORE?

More about Mandela ☆ www.nelsonmandela.org/content/page/biography

OUCH! WHY DO I SUDDENLY FEEL SO-O SLEEPY...?

Elephant gun
The vet or a ranger in a helicopter or jeep uses a high-powered rifle to fire a tranquiliser dart into the elephant's hide. The drugs from the dart can take 5 to 15 minutes to work, so the elephant has to be followed as it thunders away.

JUMBO VET

How do you stop 6 tonnes (6.6 tons) of rampaging elephant powering through the African bush at a speed of up to 40km/h (25mph)? This is just one of many problems a wildlife vet in Africa has to face in order to save animal lives.

SLEEPING GIANT

This elephant has been darted as part of a Kenyan study to map where elephants move throughout the year.

Ears are folded over eyes to protect them.

AFRICAN ELEPHANT

⭐ **Maximum weight:**
6.3 tonnes (7 tons)

⭐ **Lifespan in the wild:**
Approximately 70 years

⭐ **Numbers:** up to 690,000 roaming in 37 African countries.

22
The number of months a mother carries a baby elephant before it's born.

Get a grip

Occasionally, even elephants need a pedicure when their nails grow too long. Rather than scissors, a great big angle grinder is needed. The sole of an elephant's foot is ridged and grooved to provide a good grip.

Getting needled

As the elephant gets sleepy, the vets land and spring into action. Blood samples are taken and the sleeping elephant is checked over. Any wounds are cleaned and patched up and sometimes injections are given to ward off disease. Finally, a reversal injection is given to jolt the elephant back to its feet.

An adult male African elephant can eat 130kg (287lb) of food a day.

Rear is spray painted with a code so that the animal can be identified from a distance.

EXCUSE ME! HE'S LANDED ON MY FOOT!

HONESTLY... THIS IS WHAT WE DO!

A GPS tracking band is fitted round the neck. It gives off a signal so that researchers can track the elephant's movements.

Bathtime!

Elephants like a good dip or a shower of water from their long 8.5-litre-capacity trunk (15 pints). Afterwards, they like to cover themselves with dust. This acts as a sunblock and repels biting insects.

WANT MORE?

An elephant's molar teeth are each the size of a brick!

GOLD RUSH!

In 1886, an incredibly rich seam of gold was found beneath Gerhardus Oosthuizen's farm in the 'Rand' – the Witwatersrand area of Transvaal, South Africa. Thousands of people flocked there in the hope of becoming rich. Many did. But George Harrison, one of the first gold finders, wasn't so lucky. He sold his claim for just £10 (US$15). Silly boy!

40,000
The number of tonnes of gold produced by South Africa's mines.

Labourers at the Grahamstown Gold Mining Company in 1888.

PAST TENTS

Large mining camps grew up in the Transvaal and, as the gold continued to be discovered, the tents soon turned to brick and concrete buildings. Johannesburg sprang up from the original mining camp to become the largest city in South Africa.

DIGGING DEEP

At first the gold was mined close to the surface. As the years passed, mines became ever deeper. Mponeng is one of the world's deepest, over 3km (2mi) beneath the Earth's surface. It takes an hour to travel down to the deepest shafts in giant steel lifts called cages.

Cramped conditions within a gold mine, 1947.

There's gold in them there hills
The Rand's gold reef stretched an incredible 400km (249mi) underneath the Transvaal. It allowed South Africa to dominate world gold production in the 20th century. In 1970, it produced 79% of all new gold. Today, that's down to 10–12%, but it's still a major player.

Deep drilling in the Mponeng Gold Mine.

I'M SURE THIS IS THE WAY OUT!

Inside the Mponeng mine
It's hot, hot, hot! The rock itself can be 60°C (140°F). Air is wafted down shafts by giant fans.

Supports help keep the 3km (2mi) of rock above the miners from collapsing and flattening them.

It's cramped, sweaty and dark. A headtorch with fresh batteries is essential.

Mineworkers handle a hefty air-powered drill to chisel away the rock.

South Africa's gold deposits were formed over 3 billion years ago.

A miner displays a newly made gold bar.

Rock and awe
As little as 10g (0.4oz) of gold is recovered from each tonne of rock mined at Mponeng. But when 6000 tonnes (6614 tons) of rock is shifted per day, that adds up to some serious bling.

Molten gold is poured into moulds.

WANT MORE?

The horn blast to signal the start of the hour-long fishing event.

FISHY FESTIVAL

Africa is home to some seriously odd competitions, from ostrich and camel racing, to kudu dung spitting – where people try to spit a pellet of gazelle poo the furthest distance. One of the strangest and most colourful of all competitions is held in north-western Nigeria in March or April.

Wardens in boats watch out for any rough stuff or cheating.

HEY! WHO BROKE MY PADDLE?

FISHING FRENZY

The Argungu Fishing Festival is a four-day celebration. It marks the end of conflict between two neighbouring kingdoms. All sorts of events are held, from archery to camel races. But the thousands who attend are waiting for the main fishing event.

FADA BING

Come the big one, some 30,000 fishermen race into the Fada River, which is packed with fish. They have just one hour to catch the biggest fish possible using their traditional hand-sewn nets.

Good gourd!
The fishermen use hollowed-out giant gourds. These act both as floats to cling on to when fishing in deeper parts of the river and as a container to keep their catch in. Known as calabashes, they can also be used to kill fish by 'calabashing' them over the head!

Net gains
The fish are weighed to find the biggest. The winner's prize varies each year. Previous prizes include £5000 (US$7500) cash, a minibus, medical insurance, an electricity generator and a motorbike – all well worth the effort!

80kg
(176lb)
The weight of the winning fish in 2004. It took four men to lift it onto the scales!

WANT MORE?

See more pictures of the festival ✯ www.irenebecker.eu/2011/01/grand-fishing

KNOW YOUR CLOTHES

Do you know your shuka from your kanga? You soon will. Although western jeans, tops and soccer shirts are worn more and more in big cities, many people throughout Africa still wear their traditional clothing for ceremonies and special days.

WRAP ARTISTS

Many peoples in Africa wear a single-layered piece of cloth known as a wrapper – pagne or kanga in some places. The cloth is wrapped around the body like a cloak or long skirt, or is more elaborately tied and worn like a toga. They are often eye-wateringly colourful and patterned.

Maasai warriors dance and jump as part of a cultural ceremony.

WE SHOULD BE WEARING JUMPERS INSTEAD OF THESE CLOAKS!

Neck and neck

Many peoples in Africa, including the Maasai and Samburu, like to accessorise their clothing with beaded necklaces. Maasai women in Kenya often wear giant, disc-shaped necklaces. Colour-coded beads show whether they're married and have children.

ABSORBING INFLUENCES

The Herero people of Namibia rock their very own mix of traditional and European. Ladies' clothing includes colourful versions of ankle-length dresses first introduced by 19th-century German missionaries. Herero hats are made of cloth rolled up to form horns, symbolising their lives as cattle farmers.

CLOAKED IN RED

Worn over the shoulder and called a shuka, these simple pieces of cotton fabric are the most important of Maasai garments. These bright cloaks are usually all, or mostly, red.

THIS ROBE AIN'T BIG ENOUGH FOR THE BOTH OF US.

A grand boubou isn't a mistake. It's a wide-sleeved robe worn by many men in west Africa. The female version is sometimes called an m'boubou.

WANT MORE?

The Baganda people make cloth from the bark of the Mutaba tree.

ROCK STARS

Throughout Africa, different peoples have worked the local rock and stone to create extraordinary structures. The Dogon, for instance, live in around 700 villages made up of caves carved into the 200km-long Bandiagara cliffs (124mi) in Mali.

Holy ground

If you couldn't travel from Ethiopia to Jerusalem on a Christian pilgrimage 800 years ago, help was at hand. King Lalibela had ten churches dug out of the hard rock to form a New Jerusalem. His widow created an 11th church, St George's. All the buildings are connected by secret underground tunnels. Cool!

LOCATION, LOCATION

The Dogon built their own extensions to the caves. These distinctive tall, square mud buildings are stacked vertically up the cliff face.

1 in 8

of the 10,000 people who live in Lalibela today are priests. It really is a holy place.

Dogon huts cling to the slopes.

BET YOU CAN'T CATCH ME!

WALKING TALL

The rocky cliffs provided a safe haven. They helped the Dogon hold onto much of their unusual culture. These Dogon stiltwalkers wear carved masks and dance on stilts in a ceremony to honour their ancestors.

A Dogon masked dancer.

Church roof at ground level carved with a distinctive cross.

Surrounding area chiselled out of red granite rock, leaving a solid block in middle.

The 12.5m-tall block (41ft) was hollowed out by hand to form the church interior, complete with rooms and statues.

Outside walls sculpted using just hammer and chisel to form steps, columns and windows.

St George's Church, Lalibela

Pointy-roofed Dogon storage huts.

On hot nights, the Dogon sleep on the top of their flat-roofed homes.

In the closet
The Dogon stored their grain in buildings with pointed thatched roofs. Dogon women had their own granary buildings where they stored their clothes and possessions – the ultimate walk-in wardrobe!

Birds'-eye view of flat-roofed Dogon homes.

WANT MORE?

Dogon rituals ☆ www.traditionscustoms.com/people/dogon

IDI AMIN DADA

You didn't have to be mad to be President of Uganda in the 1970s, but it helped! Army officer Idi Amin Dada (c.1925–2003) seized power in 1971 and presided over a reign of terror, tragedy and madness that finally ended in 1979.

Amin wearing medals he gave to himself.

BRITISH LINKS

Amin joined the British army as an assistant cook in 1946. He returned to Uganda in 1959, three years before it gained independence from Britain. For a while he retained a fondness for Britain. In 1974, he started a Save Britain Fund (it raised less than £2000).

Amin dives fully clothed into a pool.

No laughing matter

Seen as a clown on the world stage, Amin was in fact a deadly and vengeful tyrant at home. He ordered the persecution of many ethnic groups that were loyal to the previous president. In his eight-year reign Amin had over 300,000 people killed.

DON'T CALL ME BONKERS!

King of Scotland

Amin's behaviour as president was often eccentric. He started wearing tartan kilts and declared himself 'King of Scotland'. He also banned hippies, and stopped women from from wearing mini skirts.

Amin became light heavyweight boxing champion of Uganda in 1951. He held the title for nine years.

Poached
Animal life suffered during Amin's reign. Three-quarters of all Uganda's elephants and nine out of ten of their rhinos were poached for ivory and horn.

WAVE YOUR HANDS IN THE AIR LIKE YOU JUST DON'T CARE.

Off you go
More than 55,000 Ugandan Asians with British passports were expelled from the country. They could only take possessions they were able to carry with them. Many owned shops and businesses that closed.

Ugandans peer into the closed shops left behind by exiled Asians.

Fall out
Amin had two-thirds of the Ugandan Army executed and replaced by his own, untrained supporters.

What's in?
It's believed that Amin kept the heads of some of his opponents in his fridge in a beach house he owned.

Name game
Most leaders are happy with 'President' or 'Prime Minister' but Amin gave himself the following official title (deep breath)…

'His Excellency President for Life, Field Marshal Al Hadji Dr Idi Amin, VC, DSO, MC, CBE, Lord of All the Beasts of the Earth and Fishes of the Sea and Conqueror of the British Empire in Africa in General and Uganda in Particular'

ALREADY DISTURBED

In exile
When Tanzania invaded Uganda in 1979, Amin fled to Libya. He then spent several years living in the whole top two floors of a posh hotel in Saudi Arabia. In return, Saudi Arabia's rulers insisted he kept out of politics.

WANT MORE?

A life in pictures ☆ www.news.bbc.co.uk/1/hi/in_depth/photo_gallery/3084491.stm

FEZ FACTS

The city of Fez was founded in 789AD and was Morocco's capital until 1912. Its medina (old walled town) has 9000 narrow streets with large souks (markets). It also has one of the world's oldest tanneries at over 800 years old.

TOUGH AS OLD BOOTS

Think your paper round in the rain is the world's worst job? You've got it easy. Check out the lot of a worker in the leather tanneries of the Moroccan city of Fez. There, you'd be working all hours preserving and colouring large, heavy leather hides by hand in a stinky fug made worse by temperatures as high as 40°C (104°F).

DYEING FOR A BREAK? A JOB TO DYE FOR... YEAH, HEARD THEM ALL BEFORE!

Stone vats filled with lime.

Tourists visiting Fez's tanneries are often given a large sprig of peppermint to sniff. This helps to ward off the strong whiff of the tanning pits.

Leather soaked in large tubs of dye.

Fabric softener

Before being dyed, the hides and skins of goats, cows and sheep are first soaked in vats of lime. Next, they're dipped in vats filled with water and a special ingredient – pigeon poo! The high ammonia content of pigeon poo makes the hides soft and supple.

Henna leaves

Poppy

Mint leaves

100 million
The number of pairs of leather slippers Morocco exports every year. What a feat!

To dye for

Different natural (henna, mint, poppy) and chemical dyes colour the leather. Sometimes, a hide will be dunked by hand into several different dyes held in stone vats to create a particular effect.

Dyed and treated hides are left to dry on the tannery roof or on nearby hill slopes.

OH DEAR, YOU'VE CAUGHT ME RED-HANDED.

SHOE IN

Once dried, the leather is cut to a pattern and turned into finished goods. These include bags, wallets, clothes and footwear, made by craftsmen in Fez and other cities of Morocco. Flat leather slippers called babouches and leather cushion seats known as pouffes are especially popular.

Hand-crafted leather pouffe

WANT MORE?

The Fez tanneries ☆ www.technologystudent.com/culture1/fez1.htm

Aerial view of the Suez Canal with the Red Sea at the bottom.

SNEAKY SHORT CUT

For many seafarers, Africa got in the way. Sailing between Europe and Asia or western North America meant making a huge detour all the way round Africa. This added thousands of kilometres to a voyage. So, when Egypt's Suez Canal opened, in 1869, it was a huge hit. It offered a sneaky short cut between southern Europe and eastern Africa and Asia.

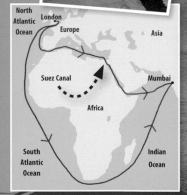

North Atlantic Ocean — London — Europe — Asia

Suez Canal — Mumbai

Africa

South Atlantic Ocean — Indian Ocean

The Suez Canal links the Mediterranean Sea to the Red Sea, which flows out into the Indian Ocean.

GRAND OPENING

The first ship through the canal was supposed to be the French yacht *L'Aigle* carrying France's Empress Eugenie. However, a Scottish sea captain George Nares had other ideas.

PLEASE DON'T MAKE US FILL IN THIS HOLE!

SUEZ CANAL CONSTRUCTION CAPERS

Canal length: 163km (101mi)
Canal width: 300m (984ft)
Construction time: 10 years
Workers: About 1.5 million
Cost: US$100 million – about US$1.7 billion (£1.1billion) today

Labourers dig out clay during the construction of the Suez Canal in Egypt, 1859.

Canal cargo
Today, about 8% of all the world's shipping passes through the Suez Canal.

250 The average number of battleships, cruisers and aircraft carriers that sail down the canal each year.

NAUGHTY NARES

The night before the opening, Captain Nares skippered his ship, HMS *Newport*, secretly ahead of all the others so that he could be first through the canal. The French were furious and Nares got an official telling off from his bosses. But he also got a pat on the back in private for winding up the French!

The official opening of the Suez Canal, 17 November 1869.

Lengthy journey
It takes around 14 hours to travel through the Suez Canal from Port Said on the Med to the port of Suez in the south.

WE'RE JUST TUGGING ALONG.

The pharaohs got there first
The genius ancient Egyptians bypassed Africa in a different way thousands of years earlier. They cut a canal between the Red Sea and the Nile River so ships could sail up Africa's east coast and into the heart of Egypt.

WANT MORE?

The Suez shortens the journey from Japan to northern Europe by 5000km (3107mi).

WASTE NOT WANT NOT

What a load of rubbish! Every day, African towns and cities generate huge amounts of solid waste. Most of this is piled up and left to rot in landfill sites or rubbish dumps. Thousands of Africans spend their lives in these dumps hunting for metals, rubber or other materials that they can sell. Others have turned waste into useful or valuable products.

Dangerous dump

Waste pickers face all kinds of hazards from razor-sharp glass and metal to breathing in toxic fumes from lethal chemicals, or being burned by leaking acids from batteries. Long-term landfill workers suffer from serious illnesses, including breathing and kidney problems.

88,000
The number of waste pickers in South Africa alone!

ANY OLD RUBBISH

The Dandora rubbish dump outside Kenya's biggest city, Nairobi, attracts up to 10,000 waste pickers. An extra 2000 tonnes (2205 tons) of rubbish is dumped at the site every day.

BOTTLE BUILDING

In 2011, a new house went up in Yelwa, Nigeria, and drew quite a crowd. It's made out of 7800 old plastic water bottles. Each one is filled with soil, stacked on top of one another and stuck in place using mud. This unique dwelling uses up waste and costs a fraction of a brick-built home.

Drumming man toy made of wire and old tin cans.

LANDFILL LOOKOUT

Items that are valuable to waste pickers include:

- Old food (to eat there and then)
- Plastic bottles
- Electronics
- Meat bones
- Rubber
- Metals

Waste pickers in Kenya may earn just £1.30 (US$2) a day for their backbreaking work.

Shoes made from rubber tractor tyres.

WHAT A LOAD OF OLD GARBAGE!

WANT MORE?

Queen of a Mali rubbish dump ☆ www.irinnews.org/Report/50295/MALI

THE GORILLA WHISPERER

In the 1960s, amateur naturalist Dian Fossey began her quest to become an expert on the mysterious mountain gorillas of Uganda, Rwanda and Congo. Captivated by their intelligence and differing personalities, Dian spent much of the rest of her life living among the gorillas in Central Africa.

I WISH I'D REMEMBERED TO BRUSH MY TEETH MORE OFTEN!

Dian Fossey with her gorilla friends in Rwanda.

Gorilla comes from the ancient Greek word 'Gorillai' which means 'tribe of hairy women'!

YOU JUST CAN'T BEAT A GOOD CUDDLE!

APING THEIR BEHAVIOUR

Fossey gained the gorillas' trust through months of sitting, moving and acting as they did. She learned to beat her chest and bellow and belch just like the gorillas. Over time, Dian was accepted by the apes and was able to hang out with them.

Standing tall

A newly born baby gorilla is super cute. It weighs around 2kg (4lb) – less than most human babies, but boy do they grow up fast. An adult male can stand almost 2m (7ft) tall and weigh more than three large men.

DEATH TRAPS

Fossey and her team in Rwanda pose beside a haul of poachers' wire snares. These could trap and kill gorillas in the forest.

Varied diet
Nettles, thistles, celery and bamboo are a few of the 100 or so plant species that gorillas gobble down. They can each chomp through 20kg (44lb) a day.

Clever monkeys
Dian learned that these super-smart primates communicated with and cared for each other. She watched them use simple tools, such as a stick, to judge the depth of a river before crossing.

Mountain gorillas can catch some human diseases and can die from the common cold.

880
The number of mountain gorillas left in the wild in 2012.

The Fossey posse
Fossey and her team fought hard to protect the gorillas from hunters, poachers and people clearing their forest habitat. Dian was killed, possibly by poachers, in Rwanda in 1985. Rangers now patrol the forests, determined to protect these magnificent creatures.

Dian was buried next to her favourite gorilla, Digit, in a gorilla graveyard in Rwanda.

WANT MORE?

Read more about gorillas ☆ www.gorillafund.org/page.aspx?pid=769

Home life

William helped his family to scrape a living by growing and harvesting groundnuts and soya beans. Their home, built of mud hardened into bricks, had no electricity. Light came from a kerosene lamp – when they could afford the fuel.

William's family home

An old bicycle provided the chain and wheel that was turned by the windmill.

BOY STORY

Unlike many kids, 14-year-old William Kamkwamba was crushed when he learned he couldn't carry on going to school. His family from Masitala, Malawi, couldn't afford the £50-a-year tuition fees (US$80). William had to stay at home instead, but his love of learning inspired him to build an extraordinary device.

Only 9% of Malawians have electricity in their homes.

Flattened-out plastic pipes formed the vanes of the windmill.

Windmill power

William loved reading at the local library. He picked up a book about energy and was fascinated to learn how windmills could generate electricity and pump water. These were the two things he thought his famine-stricken village needed most. So he set about building his very own windmill.

An old car battery stored electricity generated by the mill.

5m-high mast (16ft) lashed together from pieces of blue gum tree.

ANYONE ELSE NEED TO PARK THEIR BIKE?

Energy invention

Neighbours thought William mad for scavenging in rubbish tips for parts. But his new windmill was a success. It could power four light bulbs at home as well as charge neighbours' mobile phones. William followed up with a water pump for his family's farm field.

Back to school

William's fame earned him funds to help pay for his education. He studied in the UK, South Africa and, from 2012, in the United Sates. He has inspired the setting up of charities to provide power and clean water to many people in Malawi and elsewhere.

William wired up his family's home using coat hangers and rubber from old sandals as simple light switches.

Pedalling this Rwandan invention produces electricity to power small lights and recharge mobile phones.

WILLIAM'S OTHER PROJECTS

☆ 12m-tall windmill (39ft)
☆ Solar water pump
☆ Radio transmitter
☆ Solar-powered electricity for six homes

William won an award for his book in 2010.

WRITE TO THE TOP

Word spread of the ingenious young William and, in 2007, he was invited to an energy conference in Tanzania. There, he used a computer and the internet for the very first time. Within two years, his book, *The Boy Who Harnessed the Wind*, became a bestseller.

WANT MORE?

Check out William's blog ☆ www.williamkamkwamba.typepad.com

EXTREME AFRICA

Extreme sports in the extreme continent? You betcha!
Africa's wide-ranging and eye-catching terrain offers
exciting challenges for many speed freaks and
adrenalin junkies. Here are some of Africa's
most X-citing events.

VICTORIAAARRRGHHH!

The world-famous Victoria Falls are a
major tourist attraction. Close by, the Falls
Bridge was the world's highest when built
in 1905. Today, its 111m (364ft) drop over
the crocodile-infested Zambezi River draws
thrill-seeking bungee jumpers.

Fifty thousand
daredevils or nutters
(you decide) take the
plunge every year.

DON'T LOOK
DOWN,
DON'T LOOK
DOWN...
GULP!

In 2012, a
22-year-old
Australian student
was lucky to survive
after her bungee rope
snapped and she was
plunged into the
wild Zambezi
River.

Bungee jumping
off Victoria
Falls Bridge.

Living on the edge
A free climber scrambles up Morocco's Atlas mountains. He uses no safety ropes or harnesses. Risky!

Behind bars
Here's your new home for an hour. Feel safe and secure? Now see what's going to be crashing into it, jaws gaping, dozens of razor-sharp teeth gnashing. Are you suddenly feeling queasy? Tough. You've already signed up.

A great white shark checks out a divers' cage.

Inflatable dinghies are tossed around in the powerful waters of the southern Nile River.

MMM, LUNCH... IF ONLY I COULD BITE THROUGH THESE BARS!

RIVER DEEP, MOUNTAIN HIGH

Africa's fast-flowing rivers, such as the southern Nile, the Congo and Zambezi, churn up wicked whitewater and rapids for brave canoeists and rafters. The continent's mountains provide climbers with challenges that are equally tough.

Eye-to-eye
Shark cage diving is a popular pastime off the coast of South Africa. Here, you can get up really close to some huge sharks, including the ultimate predator, the great white. What a gut-churning experience!

DIVE N' IRON

In 2006, Louise Trewavas dived to a depth of 137m (449ft) near Dahab, Egypt. She pulled out an ironing board and performed the deepest-ever example of extreme ironing.

WANT MORE?

Extreme sports in Africa ☆ www.extremesportsguide.co.za

GLITTERING PRIZE

In 1905, Frederick Wells, the supervisor of the Premier mine in South Africa, came across an extraordinary object. At first it was thought too large to be a diamond and was nearly thrown away. It turned out to be the largest diamond ever discovered and was named after the owner of the mine, Sir Thomas Cullinan.

WILL YOU MARRY ME?

Miner holding Cullinan diamond.

YOU'VE GOT MAIL

In 1907, amidst much excitement, bystanders watched security guards board a steamboat that was bound for Britain. The guards carried a fake diamond as a decoy. The real diamond was actually sent by regular registered parcel post using a three-shilling (15p) stamp. Imagine receiving that through your letterbox!

Generous gift
The South African government bought the diamond for £150,000 (US$225,000) and gave it as a present to King Edward VII of Britain.

3106.75
The number of carats the Cullinan diamond weighed. A 1-carat diamond weighs 0.2 grams. The Cullinan weighed 621g (1lb)!

Diamond deception
The Cullinan went on another outlandish journey from London to a diamond cutter in Amsterdam. A large Royal Navy ship appeared to carry the diamond in high security to the Netherlands. But the owner of the diamond cutting company actually took it home in his pocket.

King George VI wearing the crown jewels.

Cutting edge

It was sweaty-palms time for master diamond cutter Joseph Asscher, who spent weeks studying the diamond. It then took him four days to cut the groove into which the knife that would split the diamond would be placed. Only trouble was, with the first hefty blow of his meaty mallet, the steel knife snapped, not the diamond!

Imperial State Crown

JEWEL IN THE CROWN

To huge relief, the diamond split cleanly on the second attempt. Many months later, it had been cut, polished and transformed into nine giant diamonds and 96 smaller gemstones.

Cullinan II

The Premier mine is still working. In 2009, a 507-carat diamond was found there. It sold the following year for a whopping £23.4 million (US$35.3 million).

Giant jewels

The biggest diamond, called Cullinan I or the Great Star of Africa, was set in the British Sovereign's Sceptre. The second largest was set in the Imperial State Crown.

British Sovereign's Sceptre

WANT MORE?

Check out more diamonds ★ www.valuablestones.com/largest_diamonds-2.htm

MEDICINE MEN AND WOMEN

An old Turkana medicine man. He wears wooden necklaces and charms to ward off evil spirits.

Feeling poorly or down in the dumps? In some parts of Africa, that means a trip to the local witch doctor, sangoma, inyanga or marabou. These are all local traditional healers, or medicine men or women. They use spells, rituals and herbal remedies to treat illnesses, and to predict fortunes, grant good luck and even find lost livestock.

Witch doctors in traditional bright clothing dance wildly to drive out unwanted spirits from the village.

SKULL STALLS
Traditional healers need to get their supplies from somewhere. Many shop at fetish markets such as this one in Bamako, Mali. The largest in Africa is the Akodessewa Fetish Market in Togo's capital city, Lomé. There, anything from monkey hands to cheetah skulls can be bought to make charms or medicine.

Tulip treatment

Modern science has proved that some traditional African treatments do work. The Ashanti healers in Ghana, for instance, spread a paste of the bark of the African tulip tree over a wound to fight off infection.

More than 3000 different plant species are used by inyangas (southern African healers) to treat illnesses.

A witch doctor displays a collection of lucky charms.

SOCCER SANGOMA

A number of African football teams employ witch doctors who might bury bones in the pitch or place a charm in their team's goal. South Africa used sangoma S'bonelo Madela at the 2010 World Cup. This colourful character (right) was a witch doctor for the Burkina Faso team which reached the final of the African Cup of Nations for the first time in 2013.

200,000

The number of traditional healers in South Africa, far more than regular medical doctors.

WANT MORE?

Traditional healer in aciton ☆ www.youtube.com/watch?v=Ug5N8vTMFo

DAM NATION

At over 6650km (4132mi) long, the Nile is the world's longest river. Every year it flooded, causing problems but also creating thick, rich sludge that helped to fertilise crops. In 1960, an audacious plan was made to put a dam across the Nile to control its waters and bring electricity to Egypt.

Vast pool
The dam created a giant 550km-long reservoir (342mi) called Lake Nasser.

The Aswan High Dam took 10 years to build. It involved over 25,000 Egyptian engineers and workers as well as support from the Soviet Union.

Aswan High Dam under construction, 1964.

ASWAN DAM DOSSIER

⭐ **Height:** 111m (364ft) – it's a whopper!

⭐ **Length:** 3830m (12,566ft) – told you it's a whopper.

⭐ **Width:** 980m (3215ft) at its base.

⭐ **Fully operational:** 1976

Water gushes from the dam.

Big benefits
The dam captures water during the floods and then releases it when there's drought. What's more, the water that flows through the dam turns turbines to generate lots of electricity. It gave many Egyptian villages electricity for the first time.

ARMLESS NOW, SOON TO BE LEGLESS!

SOS – save our statues
Two giant stone temples built for Pharaoh Ramesses II over 3200 years ago were going to drown in Lake Nasser until UNESCO stepped in. The temples and statues were cut into giant 20-tonne-stone blocks (22 tons). These were then moved and reassembled 65m (213ft) higher up the cliff, above the water level.

10%
of all Egypt's electricity is produced by the Aswan High Dam.

NOT ALL GOOD
More than 110,000 Egyptians and Sudanese had to move after their lands were submerged by the dam. Some farmers along the Nile complained about the loss of the fertile sediment that the yearly flood used to deposit. But other parts of Egypt have been turned from desert into lush farmlands using irrigation.

Building blocks
It would take 17 Great Pyramids from Giza to equal the amount of rock and material used to build the gigantic Aswan High Dam.

WANT MORE?

A closer look ☆ www.geography.howstuffworks.com/africa/the-aswan-dam.htm

REBELLION!

Imagine being snatched from your home country, crammed onto a ship in chains and sailed to another continent to be sold as a slave. That was the fate of 53 Africans from Sierra Leone, held aboard a ship cruising the coast of Cuba in 1839. The ship's name was *Amistad*, meaning friendship in Spanish – but things were far from friendly on board!

Several of the slaves had been flogged and had vinegar and gunpowder rubbed into their wounds. Owww!

MUTINY BELOW

The slaves found a nail below decks which they used to free themselves from their chains. Led by Sengbe Pieh (later known as Joseph Cinqué) they headed up on deck, battled the slave traders and gained control of the ship.

The slave mutiny on board the Amistad, off the coast of Cuba.

WRONG WAY

The slaves spared some of the crew, who they asked to sail them back to Sierra Leone. The crew pretended to do just that but sneakily headed northwards instead. The ship sailed for seven weeks, with food running out, until it was seized off the coast of New York City.

Slaves working on a West Indian plantation.

1.2 million

Africans are estimated to have died aboard Atlantic slave ships.

MILLIONS IN MISERY

The *Amistad* was just a tiny part of a shockingly huge trade in black Africans as slaves. Around 12 million Africans were captured and transported across the Atlantic between the 16th and 19th centuries. Most were sold as slaves to work on farms and plantations.

THIS HAS REALLY CAPTURED MY ATTENTION.

A painting of the *Amistad* trial.

COURT OUT

The slaves were charged with murder and piracy. In 1841, the case went to the US Supreme Court where the slaves were defended by former US president John Quincy Adams. He defended their right to fight to regain their freedom and won!

Money was raised to return the 35 surviving Africans to Sierra Leone aboard a ship called Gentleman.

WANT MORE?

Africans were taken as slaves to America as early as 1503.

> I'LL NEVER LEARN ALL MY LINES IN AN HOUR!

Learning lines quickly.

Shooting in a real hotel.

WELCOME TO NOLLYWOOD

After Bollywood in India, which country's film industry makes the most movies per year? Go on, have three guesses. And no, it's not the United States with Hollywood. It's Nigeria. Here, the Nollywood film industry makes and releases more than 200 movies each and every month!

Nigerian actor Gbenga Richards has his face painted.

LIGHTS, CAMERA, LAGOS

Lagos is the fastest-growing city in Africa and the first to get its own Monopoly set. It also happens to be the centre of Nollywood, with hundreds of film producers and thousands of actors and technical staff making movies as quickly and cheaply as possible.

On location in the jungle.

A political thriller is filmed.

£15,000 (US$23,040) is the cost of a typical Nollywood movie – about half a second's worth of a Hollywood hit.

Fast films

Most Nollywood movies are filmed on digital video out and about on city streets or in the Nigerian countryside. Hotel rooms and cars are hired by the day, or even the hour, to film the scene as quickly as possible to save money.

Films are usually edited on a laptop, so forget big special effects. You may see plenty of 'blood' bags full of red paint or sauce, though!

A store selling the latest Nollywood films.

Popular themes in Nigerian movies

☆ RAGS TO RICHES TALES

☆ ROMANCE AND RELATIONSHIPS

☆ BETRAYAL AND REVENGE

☆ PLIGHT OF THE POOR

☆ WITCHCRAFT AND ZOMBIES

Straight to video

Movies rarely make it to the cinema. Instead, they're sold on DVD for about £1 (US$2) each. Film stores and massive movie markets on Lagos Island and in the city of Onitsha may sell 50,000–200,000 copies of a new movie in its first week of release.

WANT MORE?

Read more ☆ www.guardian.co.uk/film/filmblog/2010/sep/21/nollywood

16 STEPS TO TREASURE TOWN!

Standing on the banks of the River Nile in 1922, archaeologist Howard Carter was staring defeat in the face. Despite many years digging at the one site, Carter had failed to unearth an ancient Egyptian pharaoh's tomb. He was about to give up when his workmen discovered 16 stone steps leading down to a doorway. What lay inside took his breath away…

Annex
The annex contained yet more stuff including board games and many of the tomb's 130 walking sticks.

Antechamber
Two life-sized models of Tutankhamun stood as sentries in the antechamber. This room contained about 700 objects including three gold couches. Sofa, so good!

Howard Carter (left) at the entrance to Tut's tomb.

Sculpture of cobra snake on forehead.

ALL THIS BLING IS HURTING MY EYES!

THE BOY-KING

The doorway led to a passage that ran into the four treasure-filled rooms of the tomb of Tutankhamun. He was the pharaoh (ruler) of Egypt more than 3300 years ago. He was just a teenager when he died.

MASK OF DEATH

Tut's magnificent death mask was made of solid gold and decorated with coloured glass and gemstones.

False beard to link pharaoh with the god Osiris.

Gilt-painted wooden ushabti.

The sarcophagus
Inside this stone sarcophagus were coffins, packed inside each other like Russian dolls.

Tomb it may concern
Many coffins contain a favourite possession of the deceased. But tombs of ancient Egyptian pharaohs went the whole hog. They had everything a pharaoh could possibly need in the afterlife. These included *ushabtis* – models of people believed to serve the dead person in the afterlife.

Model of a boat found in a tomb.

TUT'S TREASURES
Amongst more than 3,000 objects discovered in Tut's tomb were:

☆ over 40 pairs of sandals

☆ 30 boomerang-like throwing sticks

☆ a tailor's dummy

☆ 116 baskets of food

☆ 30 jars of wine

☆ a chariot

Burial chamber
The burial chamber was covered with paintings depicting the pharaoh's short life.

Treasury room
The treasury room was packed with gold statues and more than a dozen model boats.

WANT MORE?

Explore Tut's tomb further ☆ www.kingtutone.com/tutankhamun/tomb

ODD JOBS

Like nature, working outdoors and meeting people? Are you patient, with a keen eye and a good set of lungs? Then being a whale crier may be just the job for you. The only problem is there's one job like this in the whole of Africa and it's already taken. Still, it's not the only odd job on the continent.

COULD SOMEONE PLEEASE SCRATCH MY CHIN?

Crying out loud
Say hello to Pasika Noboba, who became Hermanus's fourth whale crier in 2008.

THERE SHE BLOWS

Hermanus in South Africa is a prime whale-watching spot and the whale crier is here to help. He gives long or short blasts on his kelp horn to alert people as to where whales can be sighted along the coast.

WHALE CRIER'S HORN GUIDE

• = short note - = long note

New Harbour	. . .
Preekstoel	. . .
Fick's Pool	- - -
Old Harbour	- . . .
Roman Rock	. . . .
Kwaaiwater	- - - -
Voëlklip	. - .

Eggs-acting work
Some ostrich ranches in Africa rely on people to watch over an ostrich's eggs and babies to avoid them being snatched by predators. You'd need both patience and quick reactions to leap into action and avoid pecks from the birds' powerful beaks.

I'VE GOT A CRACKING HEADACHE!

Newly hatched ostrich chick.

SNAKE MILKER

Snake milkers handle deadly poisonous snakes. They pull back their jaws and get them to secrete their venom into a jar or test tube. It's risky but important work, as the venom is used to help make snake bite antidotes.

£1100
(US$1687)
The cost of 1g (0.03oz) of some snake species' venom.

A large dose of venom from a black mamba snake, found throughout much of sub-Saharan Africa, can kill a human in just 30 minutes.

Black mamba

WANT MORE?

See the whale crier in action ☆ www.youtube.com/watch?v=--Qmmt98nyw

Don't make me angry
Even the locals reckon the Skeleton Coast is harsh. The San bushmen called it 'The Land God Made in Anger'.

IT'S BEEN A LONG DAY... I FEEL WRECKED!

Shifting sands
Some shipwrecks are now more than 60m (197ft) inland because the dunes build up and creep out into the ocean.

THE COAST OF LIFE AND DEATH

Mist rolls in along the Skeleton Coast.

Life's a beach, eh? Especially for the sailors of over 1000 different ships and boats which have been wrecked along Namibia's Atlantic coastline. Portuguese sailors, who were the first from Europe to sail there, called it the 'Coast of Death'. Today, the northern part is known as the Skeleton Coast after the remains of shipwrecks and whale skeletons that litter its beaches.

NO CHANCE

Thick fogs, the treacherous Benguela ocean current and unseen rocks that could slash through ship hulls were constant dangers to ships sailing in the past. If the ships made it ashore, sailors had little hope of survival as there were few settlements and only the hostile Namib Desert inland.

Fog survival

The thick fogs contain water vapour which provides moisture for the few plants and animals. Most life on the Skeleton Coast is found at Cape Cross, home to a huge colony of around 100,000 seals.

Oops... make that 99,999 as this black-backed jackal is likely to snatch a seal pup anytime soon!

Hot and thirsty

Gemsboks stop sweating so they can survive weeks without a drink. Their body temperature can heat up to 45°C (113°F) without damage.

Some desert beetles bask in the fog, collecting vapour droplets on their bodies which roll off into their mouths.

SURE, I CAN KEEP UP... NO SWEAT!

Welwitschia growing in Damarland, Namibia.

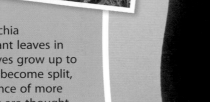

Long lifers

Found only along an 800km (497mi) stretch of the Skeleton Coast is one of the world's strangest plants. The welwitschia sprouts just two giant leaves in its lifetime. The leaves grow up to 4m (13ft) long and become split, giving the appearance of more leaves. Some plants are thought to be almost 2000 years old!

5mm
(0.2in)
The average amount of rainfall the driest parts of the Namib Desert receive.

WANT MORE?

Skeleton Coast slideshow ☆ www.on-the-matrix.com/africa/skeleton_coast.asp

INDEX

NOT FOR PARENTS
AFRICA
EVERYTHING YOU EVER WANTED TO KNOW

1st Edition
Published September 2013

WELDONOWEN

Conceived by Weldon Owen in partnership with Lonely Planet
Produced by Weldon Owen Limited
An imprint of Red Lemon Press Limited
Northburgh House,
10 Northburgh Street
London, EC1V 0AT, UK
© 2013 Weldon Owen Limited

Project managed and commissioned by Dynamo Ltd
Project manager Alison Gadsby
Project editor Gaby Goldsack-Simmonds
Designer Richard Jewitt
Picture researcher Sarah Ross
Indexer Marie Lorimer

Published by
Lonely Planet Publications Pty Ltd ABN 36 005 607 983
90 Maribyrnong St, Footscray, Victoria 3011, Australia

ISBN 979-1-74321-909-6

Printed and bound in China by 1010 Printing Int Ltd
9 8 7 6 5 4 3 2 1

All rights reserved. No part of this publication may be reproduced, stored
in a retrieval system or transmitted in any form by any means, electronic,
mechanical, photocopying, recording or otherwise, except brief extracts
for the purpose of review, without the written permission of the publisher.

Lonely Planet and the Lonely Planet logo are trademarks of Lonely Planet
and are registered in the US Patent and Trademark Office and in other
countries. Lonely Planet does not allow its name or logo to be
appropriated by commercial establishments, such as retailers, restaurants
or hotels. Please let us know of any misuses: www.lonelyplanet.com/ip

Disclaimer
Although Weldon Owen Limited and Lonely Planet have taken all
reasonable care in gathering information for this title, we make no
warranty about the accuracy or completeness of its content and, to the
extent permitted, disclaim all liability. Wherever possible, we will
endeavour to correct any errors of fact at reprint.

www.redlemonpress.com

Red Lemon Press Limited is part of
the Bonnier Publishing Group
www.bonnierpublishing.com

Credits and acknowledgments
KEY – tl top left, tc top centre, tr top right, cl centre left, c centre,
cr centre right, bl bottom left, bc bottom centre, br bottom right.

All images © Shutterstock except:

14cl, 14bl, 14cr, 15cr, 40bl, 52bl, 54bl, 59c, 68bl, 69bl, 70tr, 70bl, 89br, 93bl
Alamy: 8tl, 8tc, 8br, 9tl, 9cl, 9cr, 9br, 10tl, 11tl, 11cr, 12bl, 13tl, 13br, 16bc,
17bl, 18cl, 18cr, 19tr, 19br, 20bl, 20br, 21cl, 23tl, 25tl, 25cl, 26tl, 27br, 28tr,
28cr, 29br, 33c, 33b, 36cr, 37tr, 37br, 37tl, 37bl, 37br, 43tl, 43bl, 44cr, 45t,
45cr, 46bl, 47cr, 49tl, 50tl, 50bl, 51cr, 52cr, 53tr, 53br, 55cl, 56tr, 56cl, 54bl,
55tl, 58tl, 58br, 59tl, 60tl, 60b, 61tl, 61tr, 61br, 62bl, 63c, 67bl, 72tl, 73cr, 77tl,
77cl, 77bl, 78cr, 80tr, 82cr, 83cl, 83tl, 83cr, 84bl, 85cl, 88c, 88cr, 92bl **Corbis:**
8tr, 13bl, 16tl, 17cl, 18bl, 19tl, 21tl, 28bl, 34tl, 36bl, 43cr, 44bl, 47tl, 54c, 64bc,
66cr, 68tl, 69tr, 75tl, 76cl, 78tl, 79cr, 82tr, 82cl, 85tr, 86bl, 87tr, 87c, 88t, 89cl,
89c, 90tr, 90cr **Getty Images;** 64tl, 64cl, 65b, 71tr, 71cl, 87cl, 90bl **Rex
Features.**

Cover illustrations by **Chris Corr**

All illustrations and maps copyright 2013 Weldon Owen Limited

...SAY GOODBYE TO THE NICE PEOPLE!

LONELY PLANET OFFICES

Australia Head Office
Locked Bag 1, Footscray, Victoria 3011
Phone 03 8379 8000 Fax 03 8379 8111

USA
150 Linden St, Oakland, CA 94607
Phone 510 250 6400 Toll free 800 275 8555 Fax 510 893 8572

UK
Media Centre, 201 Wood Lane, London W12 7TQ
Phone 020 8433 1333 Fax 020 8702 0112

lonelyplanet.com/contact

MIX
Paper from
responsible sources
FSC™ C021741